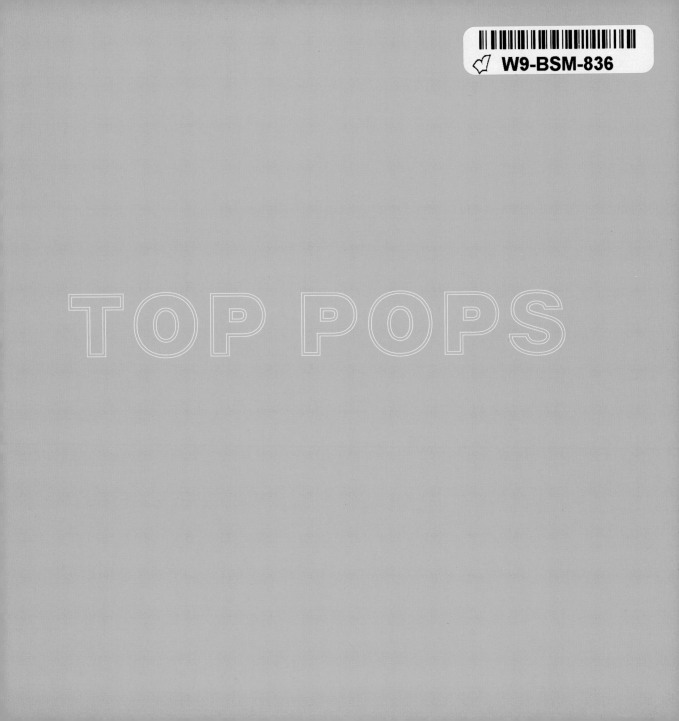

TOP POPS

TOP POPS

55 *all-natural*
FROZEN TREATS
TO MAKE AT HOME

by Emily Zaiden of The Popshop

St. Martin's Griffin

TABLE OF CONTENTS

THE POPSHOP PHILOSOPHY

Not counting the orange and apple juice pops I made with my health nut mom when I was little, I started making ice pops several summers ago, at the height of a major heat wave.

I was going to a friend's house for dinner. Dessert had to be something frozen that would keep us cool. It was the perfect moment to try out some pop molds I found in a little store near my house. Instead of a standard run-of-the-mill pop flavor, I wanted to make something a little special for my foodie friends. Something light with tang, not excessively sweet, and palate cleansing seemed ideal, so I tried out a lemon ginger combo and poured it into the molds, wondering how it would turn out. Everyone loved them. Sucking away, we talked about other fun flavors to experiment with. I couldn't wait to try out more.

Soon, I couldn't stop experimenting. The possibilities for flavor combinations seemed endless. I played with ingredients, molds, and even freezing methods. A friend and I even tried to brine freeze the pops in huge vats of salt water. What a lesson that was!

Along with the experiments came a lot of taste testing. I had friends try several recipe variations and all kinds of flavor combos and they would rank their favorites. This went on for several months and then all of a sudden, sitting at my desk at work on yet another slow day, I realized I had to do something with these ice pops. A farmers' market seemed like the best place to debut my experiments. Why not? The Popshop was born.

My goal was to make grown-up pops using the finest seasonal, local produce and in a range of sophisticated flavors. We are so lucky to have such a huge range of incredible fruits and herbs at our fingertips in California. Anything local and fresh always has the strongest and clearest flavor, so I wanted to stick with ingredients from local farms as much as possible. I also wanted to have a positive impact on the environment by not requiring that my food be shipped from all over the world. In addition, organic food isn't an option anymore; it's a necessity if you want to avoid pesticides for your own health and the planet's, so the pops are made of organic ingredients.

Coming up with the flavors was and is one of the best parts of the process. I went for new spins on classic flavors, like strawberry lemonade and orange pineapple, as well as fresh innovations like lemon basil and avocado vanilla. I wanted to make pops for the traditionalists among us (and, of course, all the kids) as well as appeal to grown-ups whose palates craved a gourmet adventure. A world of frozen delights opened up to me.

From my stand at the farmers' market, I soon learned that kids are the biggest ice pop fiends. I've had the honor and privilege of serving several first ice pops. It's pretty funny to watch the first lick, the surprise at how cold it is, and then the slow awareness that there is something sweet and tasty there that should be crammed into one's face as swiftly and efficiently as possible. I think a few toddlers made me their hero when I rescued them from the torture of teething with these frozen delights.

Other kids, some of them budding foodies, were always excited to see if their favorite flavors were on tap for the day. One of my favorite four-year-old customers got so hooked on rhubarb, mainly because it was a new word for him, that he and his dad baked me a rhubarb pie at home to thank me. For the recipes in this book and the Popshop overall, what you see is what you get. They are 100 percent natural. Unlike the stuff on store shelves, these have no dyes, stabilizers, or additives. Nothing beats the natural color and flavor of the fruit. I firmly believe kids can learn to prefer the look and taste of natural ice pops instead of the glow-in-the-dark, stain-your-tongue versions.

The recipes are designed not to be cloyingly sweet. It's a conservative take on sugar, opting for tangy and tart as much as possible and letting the flavor of the fruit, the spices, or the cocoa shine through. I like to keep the flavor combos fairly simple, doing just enough to create flavors that are out of the ordinary, but not so complex that you can't taste all of the ingredients. The flavors I share here span a broad range of preferences and types of pops—I hope there is something for everybody.

I've tried to make things as easy and simple as possible so that even if you're not an expert in the kitchen, you can make pops all the time. I hope you will! My wish is that you will be inspired to try your own frozen experiments—and enjoy the process.

—*Emily Zaiden*

FLAVOR INSPIRATIONS TO MIX AND MATCH

The diverse culinary world of Los Angeles is a big source of inspiration for the Popshop flavor pairings. I can pretty much find any bizarre, exotic food in just a short jaunt from my home. I get inspired by the fantastic food markets and independent specialty grocery shops we have.

I also like looking at desserts globally to inspire great ideas. Thinking about the incredible treats I've had on my travels provides flavor inspiration that I try to encapsulate in my pops. The food and drinks you love are a great place to start when dreaming up the perfect pop.

It's easy to go crazy with experimental ingredients, so allow yourself some trial and error. That's the fun of it!

SUGGESTIONS TO GET YOU STARTED:

- Chocolate can stand its ground. It can handle the bitterness of coffee and the kick of chili.

- Think about more than dessert flavor combinations as your muse; sauces and seasonings can be adapted, like lemon rosemary or basil lime.

- Spicy goes where it's hot. Chili is great with tropical fruits like mango and pineapple.

- Stick within a season with your flavor pairings. Heavier, wintery spices go nicely with winter fruits, such as clove and cranberry.

- Pair your herbs with fruits that ripen during the same season. Lemon verbena is lovely with peaches at the height of summer.

- Combine flavors as they are paired by cultural tradition, like pomegranate with rose water and coffee with cardamom.

- Lemon and lime are great bases for many pop flavors. They are fairly neutral, though lime is more distinct and bitter than lemon. They just don't fit well with the two main creamy bases, chocolate and vanilla.

- Keep it local for safe bet combos. Limes go best with fruits and flavors from more tropical places where they are more common than lemons, which go best with Mediterranean flavors.

- Get inspired by your favorite cocktails and drinks. Cosmopolitan or Fuzzy Navel, anyone? Or how about a green tea latte pop?

- You generally can't go wrong when mixing florals with citrus. Rose and lavender are nice with orange, lemon, and lime.

SEASONAL FLAVORS CHART

Starting with the freshest local produce always makes pops more flavorful, colorful, and healthier. The shorter the distance a fruit has to travel, the stronger the flavor. All of my recipes are created with the fundamental theory that each pop should taste like the flavor it is named for, not just like sugar. By sticking with what's available seasonally and locally, you will start out ahead of the game.

Below is a general guide to what's in season, but be sure to check the farmers' markets in your area since crops will vary depending on your region. If you're lucky enough to live in California, where the growing season is long, you have access to many of these fruits throughout the year.

WINTER	SPRING	SUMMER	FALL
Avocado	Apricot	Basil	Apple
Blood orange	Cherry	Blackberry	Cara Cara orange
Clementine orange	Mint	Blueberry	Cranberry
Grapefruit	Rhubarb	Boysenberry	Grape
Guava	Strawberry	Cantaloupe	Kiwi
Kumquat	Valencia orange	Cherry	Lime
Lemon		Cucumber	Mandarin orange
Minneola		Fig	Pear
Navel orange		Honeydew	Persimmon
Passion fruit		Lemon verbena	Pomegranate
Pomelo		Lychee	Pumpkin
Tangelo		Mango	
		Nectarine	
		Papaya	
		Peach	
		Plum	
		Raspberry	
		Watermelon	

TIPS AND TECHNIQUES

FILLING THE MOLDS Remember to leave a little room at the top of each mold for the displacement that happens when you add the handle or stick. Also, the liquid will expand slightly once it is frozen, so that extra room comes in handy.

EXTRACTION Pulling pops out of molds is harder than it seems. A lot depends on how hard the pops have frozen, which depends on the temperature they freeze at, and the ingredients in the liquid. It's best to always let pops freeze as long as possible. When you're ready to pull them out, the key is to be swift once they are ready to release. Timing this is a delicate science that takes practice, especially when you're pulling out the softer, creamy pops that can sometimes break in the mold.

Here are the basics: Take the mold out of the freezer and let thaw for a minute. Then, run it under warm water for a few seconds to loosen the pop. Try not to spin the handle or stick because this weakens the way it bonds with the pop and you'll wind up breaking the pop and pulling out the handle or stick. Pull strongly on the handle or stick but never force it. If the pop isn't ready to come out, just wait a minute and try again until it comes out easily.

MAKING MULTILAYERED POPS These are more time-consuming than single-flavor pops because you have to wait for each layer to freeze solid before you move on. Other than requiring time and patience, they're not that difficult to prepare and adults are just as wowed by these as kids.

SUSPENDED TREATS You can add pieces of fruit, chocolate chips, or other edible surprises that fit whatever recipe you are working on. Unless you are using one of the thicker, creamy recipes, added treats tend to float up to the top of the mold cavity. To avoid this, wait until pops are slushy and partially frozen to add the extra ingredients.

SERVING AND DISPLAY Here again, the recipe can inspire bold choices. Moroccan glasses are elegant for Turkish coffee pops. Or espresso cups for mocha pops. Treat the pops like you would any elegant dessert or appetizer. Just serve them swiftly before they melt, or put them on a bed of dry ice.

WRAPPING AND STORING You might want to wrap your pops to give them as gifts or bring to parties. Check a local craft or hobby shop for candy-wrapping supplies that can double as pop wrappers. You can usually find cellophane sleeve wrappers in these stores. Close them by using bright ribbons or twist ties or colorful tape. Always wrap them close to when they will be served so that they stay fresh and free of frost.

If you need to store your pops outside the molds, use tightly sealed freezer containers or freezer bags.

SELECTING INGREDIENTS

CHOCOLATE AND COCOA Select a powder with the richness and sweetness you desire. The right bitterness is key, but you don't want it to get chalky. Dutch-process dissolves nicely, but natural can work. I like the finer brands such as Valrhona and Scharffen Berger.

MILK Popshop pops started out vegan and dairy-free. Since then I've added several cows' milk recipes to the repertoire where it works best for texture and flavor. Soy, almond, coconut, rice, or other nondairy milk can be substituted pretty much interchangeably in most recipes, with only slight changes to flavor and sweetness. Soy and coconut milk are the creamiest of the nondairy options, while rice milk is the lightest, basically the equivalent of nonfat cows' milk. Whole milk gives pops a more creamy and thick texture, but low fat milk is a compromise that cuts down the fat content. Nonfat can also be used, but it definitely makes pops a little icier. Whatever you choose, organic is preferred.

SUGAR Popshop pops are made with organic cane sugar. I try to keep the added sugar to a minimum and think the taste is ideal, but alternatives also work. I use only natural alternative sweeteners.

AGAVE NECTAR This can be used instead of sugar. There has been controversy about how healthy it really is and there are issues about the quality of certain brands. Generally, agave is good for certain recipes, but since it is syrupy, too much can affect how solidly the pop freezes. For the best results, use it for recipes that require less added sweetener.

STEVIA Another sugar alternative, stevia works well in terms of consistency and texture. Boil the leaves and make a liquid, or use a premade powder version, which is fine depending on how it's processed and provided it doesn't have many additives. Stevia does have a distinct aftertaste, though, that not everyone likes.

SPICES It's always best to grind your own whole spices. You can use a coffee grinder. Just wipe it out before and after you use it so as not to mix the flavors.

ORANGE BLOSSOM WATER AND ROSE WATER These are found at specialty gourmet markets, often at fine liquor stores since they are used in mixed drinks, and at Middle Eastern and Indian grocery shops. If you can't find it near you, the Internet is always your friend. Buy it online.

CREAMSICLES &
PUDDING POPS

APRICOT HONEY YOGURT

BANANAS FOSTER

BANANA CHOCOLATE

MEXICAN FUDGESICLE

CHOCOLATE MALT

BROWN SUGAR STRAWBERRY KEFIR

BLACK CHERRY YOGURT

AVOCADO VANILLA

APRICOT HONEY YOGURT

INGREDIENTS
(Makes 10–12 three-ounce pops)

3 cups low fat plain yogurt

¾ cup apricot preserves

¼ cup honey

One of my favorite farmers added a beehive to her citrus farm a couple of years ago and started producing the most delicious orange blossom honey. She taught me a lot about the plight of the bees, who've have had such a tough time in recent years. I think we should start using more honey, along with all the other environment-friendly essentials, to help increase bee populations across the country. Plus, honey has lots of vitamins and nutrients, especially when raw, so that's a great bonus.

Use high-quality, local honey from a respected beekeeper for the best results and the strongest flavor. The tang of the yogurt is the perfect contrast to the honey's sweetness.

PREPARATION

- In a blender, pour the yogurt, preserves, and honey. Blend on high for 30 seconds, or until ingredients are fully incorporated.

- Pour the mixture into molds, insert mold handles, and place in the freezer. If using sticks, insert them after 15 minutes or when the mixture is firm enough for them to stand upright. Freeze until solid, 4 to 5 hours minimum.

TIP
To get the honey to blend well, you can thin it out a bit by stirring in one teaspoon of boiling water.

BANANAS FOSTER

INGREDIENTS
(Makes 10–12 three-ounce pops)

4 very ripe to overripe bananas, peeled and chopped

2 cups rice milk or low fat milk

1 teaspoon cinnamon

½ teaspoon nutmeg

½ teaspoon cloves

2 tablespoons vanilla extract

2 tablespoons rum extract

6 tablespoons sugar

Dash of sea salt

This pop pays homage to the classic retro-Americana dessert, a favorite of my banana-loving brother-in-law. The mixture makes a delicious banana smoothie by itself. You can also use real rum instead of extract if authenticity is important, or if you're feeling feisty.

The added beauty of this pop is that if you want to be extra healthy, you can skip the sugar since the overripe bananas will be sweet enough on their own. The sprinkle of sea salt gives the pop a hint of caramel flavor.

PREPARATION

- In a blender, add the bananas, rice milk, cinnamon, nutmeg, cloves, vanilla extract, rum extract, sugar, and salt. Blend on high until the bananas are emulsified and the mixture is creamy and even.

- Pour the mixture into molds, insert mold handles, and place in the freezer. If using sticks, insert them after 15 minutes or when the mixture is firm enough for them to stand upright. Freeze until solid, 4 to 5 hours minimum.

BANANA CHOCOLATE

A perfect combination: this version starts with rich, dark cocoa that is bitter enough to balance the sweetness of the bananas. For a fun twist, do a two-tone version by adding a layer of Bananas Foster (see previous page).

PREPARATION

- In a medium saucepan on low heat, add milk and whisk in cocoa powder, vanilla extract, and sugar. Whisk vigorously as the milk simmers to eliminate any lumps. Make sure the sugar has completely dissolved and the liquid is well blended. Remove from heat and let cool before the mixture boils and begins to reduce.

- In a blender, add the bananas. Pour the lukewarm cocoa mixture over the bananas and blend for 30 seconds or until the bananas are smoothly blended and there are no longer any chunks. Let the mixture rest until any froth has dissipated, or remove the froth by spooning it off.

- Pour the mixture into molds, insert mold handles, and place in the freezer. If using sticks, insert them after 15 minutes or when the mixture is firm enough for them to stand upright. Freeze until solid, 4 to 5 hours minimum.

INGREDIENTS
(Makes 8–10 three-ounce pops)

2 cups milk

¼ cup unsweetened Dutch-process cocoa powder

½ teaspoon vanilla extract

⅓ cup sugar

4 very ripe bananas, peeled and chopped

MEXICAN FUDGESICLE

Chocolate was blended with spices and served as a drink in the ancient Mesoamerican cultures that first discovered the cacao tree. Mexican hot chocolate and other drinks such as champurrado *are modern versions of that earlier tradition. When it comes to chocolate in any form, I prefer dark to milk, so I say the more cocoa, the merrier. This recipe keeps the pops sweet enough that milk chocolate lovers will love this one, too.*

PREPARATION

- In a medium saucepan on low heat, pour the milk and whisk in the cocoa, sugar, cinnamon, nutmeg, and all-spice. Whisk vigorously as the milk comes to a simmer to eliminate any lumps. Make sure the sugar has completely dissolved and the mixture is well blended. Remove from heat before the mixture boils and begins to reduce. Let cool for a few minutes, and then pour the mixture through a fine-mesh strainer into a medium bowl to remove the spice grains.

- Let the mixture chill in the refrigerator for 30 minutes and pour into molds. Insert mold handles and place in the freezer. If using sticks, insert them after 15 minutes or when the mixture is firm enough for them to stand upright. Freeze until solid, 4 to 5 hours minimum.

INGREDIENTS
(Makes 10–12 three-ounce pops)

4 cups whole or soy milk

¾ cup unsweetened Dutch-process cocoa powder

¾ cup sugar

1 tablespoon cinnamon

1 teaspoon nutmeg

½ teaspoon allspice

TIP
Add a dash of chili powder to this recipe to give it an extra kick. The cold but spicy sensation is fantastic. You can use cinnamon sticks instead of wooden sticks if you really want to wow your friends.

CHOCOLATE MALT

INGREDIENTS

(Makes 8 three-ounce pops)

3 cups whole milk

½ cup unsweetened Dutch-process cocoa powder

1 teaspoon vanilla extract

½ cup sugar

½ cup malted milk powder

I inherited my mom's weakness for chocolate-covered malt balls. Believe it or not, malt powder, made of wheat and malted barley, dates to the 1880s, when it originated as a health food supplement for infants. Midwestern drugstores, such as Walgreens, popularized malted milkshakes in the 1920s and they took off. It's hard to find a quality malt powder in this day and age. Most of them are super sweet and not all that flavorful. Horlick's, which was the first brand in the United States, is still one of the best if you can find it.

PREPARATION

• In a medium saucepan on low heat, pour milk and whisk in cocoa powder, vanilla extract, and sugar. Whisk vigorously as the milk simmers to eliminate any lumps. Make sure the sugar has completely dissolved and the liquid is well blended. Remove from heat before the mixture boils and begins to reduce, and whisk in the malted milk powder until fully incorporated. Let mixture chill in the refrigerator for about 30 minutes.

• Remove the mixture from the refrigerator and stir in case any separation has occurred. Pour into molds, insert handles, and place in the freezer. If using sticks, insert them after 20 minutes or when the mixture is firm enough for them to stand upright. Freeze until solid, 4 to 5 hours minimum.

BROWN SUGAR STRAWBERRY KEFIR

Kefir is an underappreciated wonder food. Now that probiotics, or beneficial microorganisms, are all the rage, kefir is beginning to take its place in the spotlight. Most supermarkets now carry it, not just the health food stores, and they even offer a few flavor and brand choices. The fruity versions are kind of like ready-made smoothies, and you can flavor plain kefir any way you want. This recipe is super easy, and super delish. You can definitely try this with the kids.

PREPARATION

- In a blender, add the kefir, preserves, and the strawberries. In a small bowl, combine the water and brown sugar and stir into a syrup or paste. Pour the sugar mixture into the blender and blend on high for 30 seconds until the mixture is smooth and even. The result should be thick but thinner than a milkshake.

- Pour the mixture into molds, insert handles, and place in the freezer. If using sticks, insert them after 15 minutes or when the mixture is firm enough for them to stand upright. Freeze until solid, 4 to 5 hours minimum.

INGREDIENTS
(Makes 8–10 three-ounce pops)

2½ cups strawberry kefir

2½ teaspoons strawberry preserves

1¼ cups halved strawberries

1 tablespoon boiling water

4½ tablespoons brown sugar

TIP

The probiotics found in yogurt and kefir aid digestion by preventing the growth of harmful bacteria in the stomach. Kefir is also a great source of protein and calcium.

BLACK CHERRY YOGURT

INGREDIENTS
(Makes 12–14 three-ounce pops)

1 cup pitted cherries

¾ cup cherry preserves

3 cups plain low fat yogurt

This is my version of a Push-up, only better. Push-ups were one of the only desserts my mom would let me have when I was little because they were slightly healthier than the other options and resembled frozen yogurt. This is definitely an upgrade in terms of pure, real ingredients. Cherries have been shown to have great antioxidant and anti-inflammatory properties. I hope my mom approves of this recipe. And it's so easy, you'll feel like you're cheating.

These have a sweet and sour tang, much like the tart frozen yogurt that has become popular at the frozen yogurt shops like Pinkberry and Yogurtland that have popped up all over Los Angeles in the past few years.

PREPARATION

- In a blender, pour all the ingredients and blend on high for 30 seconds. The mixture should be evenly but coarsely blended with some cherry bits swirled throughout. For a smoother texture, continue blending to your taste.

- Pour the mixture into molds, insert handles, and place in the freezer. If using sticks, insert them after 15 minutes or when the mixture is firm enough for them to stand upright. Freeze until solid, 4 to 5 hours minimum.

AVOCADO VANILLA

I really wasn't an avocado-holic until I came across my first avocado shake in a Filipino restaurant. Like most Americans, I never thought of avocado as a dessert, although much of the world begs to differ. Most countries in Southeast Asia, from Vietnam to Indonesia and Bali, as well as Brazil and other parts of the world, embrace the sweeter side of the avocado. I even managed to convert several avocado farmer friends from being strict savory purists to loving them as a dessert with this recipe.

Thanks to all those good fats, the richness of avocado can't be beat for creamy desserts. This is a perfect treat for sneaking in great vitamins and nutrients for kids. Call it "green vanilla" and you'll see.

PREPARATION

- Slice the avocados in half and remove the pits. With a large spoon, scoop out the flesh, scraping out as much of the bright green flesh near the skin as possible. This green will give the pop a creamy, earthy tone. In a blender, add the avocado, vanilla extract, milk, and sugar. Blend on high until the mixture is smooth and evenly mixed.

- Pour the mixture into molds, insert handles, and place in the freezer. If using sticks, insert them after 15 minutes or when the mixture is firm enough for them to stand upright. Freeze until solid, 4 to 5 hours minimum.

INGREDIENTS

(Makes 10–12 three-ounce pops)

2 ripe, unblemished Hass avocados

1½ tablespoons vanilla extract

3 cups rice milk or nonfat milk

¾ cup sugar

TIP

These pops are great for vegans and others avoiding dairy, since the avocado provides all the creaminess that nondairy ice cream alternatives often don't have.

FRUITY & FRESH POPS

POMEGRANATE ORANGE ROSE

KIWI CLEMENTINE

BLOOD ORANGE

BROWN SUGAR RUBY GRAPEFRUIT

STRAWBERRY RHUBARB

BLACKBERRY LIME VERBENA

INGREDIENTS

(Makes 8–10 three-ounce pops)

1 cup fresh-squeezed orange juice

2 cups pure pomegranate juice, preferably fresh

2 teaspoons rose water

3 tablespoons sugar

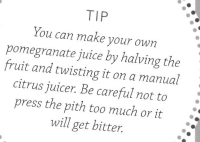

TIP

You can make your own pomegranate juice by halving the fruit and twisting it on a manual citrus juicer. Be careful not to press the pith too much or it will get bitter.

POMEGRANATE ORANGE ROSE

This is an intoxicating combination of flavors. The super food pomegranate is complemented by a touch of citrus and a hint of rose. As one of the most ancient cultivated fruits, there is so much history, mythology, and symbolism tied to pomegranates. They were said to have grown in the Garden of Eden and scholars think it might have been one of these that actually tempted Eve—does it get any more romantic than that? They are also high in vitamin C and antioxidants, so they help protect cells from damage and may fight heart disease and cancer.

Rose water is sold at Middle Eastern and Indian grocery shops. You can also find it at fine liquor stores because it is used in cocktails.

PREPARATION

* In a blender, pour all the ingredients and blend on high until the sugar has completely dissolved. The liquid should be evenly mixed, with a deep scarlet rose color. Let the mixture rest until any froth has dissipated, or remove the froth by spooning it off.

* Pour the mixture into molds, insert handles, and place in the freezer. If using sticks, insert them after 15 minutes or when the mixture is firm enough for them to stand upright. Freeze until solid, 4 to 5 hours minimum.

KIWI CLEMENTINE

This tangy combination is packed with vitamins and flavor. The kiwi seeds fleck the green pops and add a slight crunch to the texture. The taste is simple and nice for kids. If you want to make it healthier for them, eliminate the sugar. They won't miss it, especially if you use kiwis and Clementine oranges that are at their prime ripeness. If you can't find good Clementines, you can substitute mandarins, tangerines, or even navel oranges. Also, using navel oranges will cut down on time, but they are generally not as sweet as a mandarin or tangerine.

PREPARATION

- Slice the kiwis in half and scoop out the flesh with a spoon, or quarter the kiwis and peel off the skins with a knife. Discard the peels. You should have 1 ½ cups of kiwis when finished. In a blender, add the kiwis and pour in the Clementine orange juice. Add the sugar and blend on high for a minute or so, until the kiwi is fully mashed and the sugar has completely dissolved. Let the mixture rest until any froth has dissipated, or remove the froth by spooning it off.

- Pour the mixture into molds, insert handles, and place in the freezer. If using sticks, insert them after 30 minutes or when the mixture is firm enough for them to stand upright. Freeze until solid, 4 to 5 hours minimum.

INGREDIENTS
(Makes 8–10 three-ounce pops)

8 kiwis

2 cups fresh-squeezed Clementine orange juice

⅓ cup sugar

BLOOD ORANGE

INGREDIENTS

(Makes 12–14 three-ounce pops)

2½ cups fresh-squeezed blood orange juice

2½ cups fresh-squeezed orange juice

Zest of 2 blood oranges

⅓ cup sugar

Blood oranges have become widely available in the United States over the last few years. Before that, I had only tasted them in Italy, where they are a ubiquitous winter citrus that grows in Sicily and has a unique intensity. They are perfect for juicing. The color of the flesh and juice, due to a pigment called anthocyanin, gives these pops a deep crimson tone.

PREPARATION

* In a blender, pour all the ingredients and blend on high until the sugar has completely dissolved.

* Pour the mixture into molds, insert handles, and place in the freezer. If using sticks, insert them after 30 minutes or when the mixture is firm enough for them to stand upright. Freeze until solid, 4 to 5 hours minimum.

TIP

Tangerine juice is a good substitute for orange juice if you want to bump up the sweetness of the pops.

BROWN SUGAR RUBY GRAPEFRUIT

These pops are great for brunches or for a quick breakfast treat before you head to work. For extra intrigue, you can add a tablespoon of ground coriander, cloves, or fennel when you blend the ingredients. If you use ruby grapefruit, you will have deep coral pops, but you can also use other grapefruit.

PREPARATION

- Halve the grapefruit. With a large citrus juicer, juice the grapefruit and retain the pulp but remove the seeds and pith. You should have 4 cups of juice and pulp when finished. In a blender, add the pulpy juice with the brown sugar and blend until the sugar has completely dissolved and the pulp is evenly blended throughout. Let the mixture rest until any froth has dissipated, or remove the froth by spooning it off.

- Pour the mixture into molds, insert handles, and place in the freezer. If using sticks, insert them after 30 minutes or when the mixture is firm enough for them to stand upright. Freeze until solid, 4 to 5 hours minimum.

INGREDIENTS
(Makes 10–12 three-ounce pops)

4 ruby grapefruit

1½ cup brown sugar

TIP
You can easily make this an adult pop by adding two tablespoons vodka or gin and calling this a Greyhound pop. Sprinkle in some salt and you've got a Salty Dog pop! Due to the alcohol content, these pops take longer to freeze.

STRAWBERRY RHUBARB

INGREDIENTS
(Makes 14–16 three-ounce pops)

4 stalks rhubarb

3 cups water

1½ cups sugar

1 cup sliced strawberries

Here again, I owe this to a farmer who couldn't get rid of his rhubarb at the farmers' market one day. I'd always loved it in pie but never thought about using these fruits as a pop. It became one of my most beloved. I adore rhubarb on its own, and it's hard for me to save enough to sell to customers. I eat the cooked mixture out of the pot.

This flavor also makes me think of one of my favorite customers, a three-year-old who got introduced to and then obsessed with rhubarb and had to have one of these every Sunday. You should have seen the look on his face when I didn't have them one morning. Don't mess with a three-year-old and his rhubarb addiction.

PREPARATION

- Rinse and chop the rhubarb into 1-inch segments. In a medium saucepan on medium-low heat, add the rhubarb, water, and sugar. Simmer 30 minutes or until the liquid has reduced and the rhubarb is mushy and stringy in a thickened, juicy liquid. Cool to room temperature. In a blender, pour the rhubarb mixture along with any juice. Add the strawberries and blend on high for 30 seconds or until the mixture is slightly thick but evenly mixed.

- Pour the mixture into molds, insert handles, and place in the freezer. If using sticks, insert them after 30 minutes or when the mixture is firm enough for them to stand upright. Freeze until solid, 4 to 5 hours minimum.

BLACKBERRY LIME VERBENA

INGREDIENTS

(Makes 8–10 three-ounce pops)

1 cup fresh lemon verbena leaves

1½ cups water

1½ cups sugar

1½ cups blackberries

⅓ cup fresh-squeezed lime juice

This is such a good one that I hate to wait for the fruit and verbena to be in season. Bursting with berries, these pops get a bright sophistication from the lemon verbena. The vibrant, lemony scent of fresh verbena is heaven, and making the syrup is part of the fun.

PREPARATION

- Roughly chop the verbena leaves. In a small saucepan on medium-low heat, add the water and sugar, and stir as the liquid comes to a simmer until the sugar is completely dissolved. Add the verbena leaves and simmer for five minutes. Remove from heat and let cool; then pour the syrup through a fine-mesh strainer into a medium bowl and discard the leaves. Refrigerate the mixture overnight.

- In a blender, add the syrup, blackberries, and lime juice. Blend on high for 30 seconds or until the liquid is completely smooth and even.

- Pour the mixture into molds, insert handles, and place in the freezer. If using sticks, insert them after 30 minutes or when the mixture is firm enough for them to stand upright. Freeze until solid, 4 to 5 hours minimum.

COFFEE & TEA POPS

THAI ICED TEA

TURKISH COFFEE

ARNIE PALMER

VIETNAMESE COFFEE

CHILLED CHAI

MOCHA

THAI ICED TEA

INGREDIENTS

(Makes 6–8 three-ounce pops)

¾ cup Thai tea leaf mix

Dash of ground cinnamon

Dash of ground star anise

Dash of ground cloves

Dash of ground allspice

¼ teaspoon orange blossom water

2 cups boiling water

¼ cup sugar

1½ tablespoons sweetened condensed milk

½ cup cream or coconut milk, plus 2 tablespoons reserved

Instead of starting from scratch with black tea, I make this with a preblended Thai tea that has all of the spices plus that crazy orange dye (you can buy it online). Even though it's against the Popshop ideology, I need that flash of color to make this one right. It's true—I will compromise all of my principles for Thai tea. If you can't find the tea mix, you can try black tea with larger amounts of spices.

PREPARATION

- In a tea press or teapot, add the tea mix, cinnamon, star anise, cloves, allspice, and orange blossom water. Pour in the water and steep for five minutes or until the liquid is deep orange. In a small pitcher, add the sugar and condensed milk. Pour the hot tea through a fine-mesh strainer into the pitcher with the sugar and condensed milk. Stir until the sugar is completely dissolved. Stir in the ½ cup of cream and chill.

- Take the molds and pour ½ teaspoon of the reserved cream into each ice pop cavity and freeze for 20 minutes. Remove the molds from the freezer and pour the tea mixture in on top of the cream to give the swirled effect of a Thai iced tea. You can also let the cream layer freeze completely, about two hours, then pour the tea mixture on top to create a solid stripe.

- Insert mold handles and place in the freezer. If using sticks, insert them after 15 minutes or when the mixture is firm enough for them to stand upright. Freeze until solid, 4 to 5 hours minimum.

TURKISH COFFEE

INGREDIENTS
(Makes 8 three-ounce pops)

4 cups cold water

6 heaping tablespoons
extra dark, very fine
ground coffee

2½ teaspoons ground
cardamom

½ cup sugar

Spiked with cardamom, these pops are a riff on the Turkish coffee tradition, which is a central part of Turkish culture. It dates back to mid-sixteenth-century Istanbul, when the Ottomans popularized the drink. It was soon introduced in Europe. These pops are robust and sweet, just like the real thing. They'll wake you up on a hot afternoon. If you're a purist, brew true Turkish coffee for these pops. If not, substitute espresso or extra strong brewed or French pressed coffee. Just be sure to add the cardamom to the ground coffee before you prepare it.

PREPARATION

- In a large saucepan, pour in the water and whisk in the coffee and cardamom. Add the sugar and stir until it dissolves. Heat the mixture slowly over medium heat. Keep whisking the mixture so that it does not boil over. After the coffee mixture boils for one minute, let it cool completely.

- Pour the mixture through a fine-mesh strainer into a pitcher and reserve the grounds. Pour the coffee into the molds. For an authentic touch, sprinkle a dash of the coffee grounds in each cavity. Just make sure to add a very small amount, because grainy pops are not very pleasant.

- Pour the mixture into molds, insert handles, and place in the freezer. If using sticks, insert them after 30 minutes or when the mixture is firm enough for them to stand upright. Freeze until solid, 4 to 5 hours minimum.

ARNIE PALMER

My sister got me hooked on Arnold Palmers, sometimes called half-and-halfs, even though we know nothing about golf. These are great for serving at summer sporting events because they are so refreshing, and the shot of caffeine is a good afternoon pick-me-up. You can use whatever tea you like for these; I prefer Earl Grey because the bergamot works so well with the lemon.

PREPARATION

* In a kettle on medium high, heat the water until it is just about to come to a boil. In a bowl, add the tea and sugar, and pour in the water. Let steep for five minutes. Remove the tea bags and stir until the sugar is completely dissolved. Stir in the lemon juice and chill the mixture in the refrigerator.

* Pour the mixture into molds, insert handles, and place in the freezer. If using sticks, insert them after 30 minutes or when the mixture is firm enough for them to stand upright. Freeze until solid, 4 to 5 hours minimum.

INGREDIENTS

(Makes 10–12 three-ounce pops)

4 cups cold water

12 Earl Grey tea bags

1¼ cups sugar

½ cup fresh-squeezed lemon juice

TIP

To make a layered pop, reduce this recipe by half and make a straight lemonade layer by blending 1 cup fresh-squeezed lemon juice, 1 cup water, and ½ cup sugar. Freeze the tea layer with wooden sticks inserted, then pour the lemonade layer on top and freeze until solid.

VIETNAMESE COFFEE

This recipe is simple but requires two essentials: dark roast French coffee (or better yet, coffee with chicory), and sweetened condensed milk. When the French colonized Vietnam and introduced coffee production in the late nineteenth century, canned milk was much more accessible than fresh because of the tropical climate. Ca phe sua da or café sua da, meaning "coffee milk ice," emerged as the national beverage.

Use a proper Vietnamese-style drip coffee-maker for this recipe. If you can't get one, espresso or even extra strong French press coffee works fine, too.

PREPARATION

- In a bowl, pour the coffee and the milk, and stir until the milk is completely blended. You can vary the amount of condensed milk, based on your sweetness preferences. Let cool to room temperature.

- Pour the mixture into molds, insert handles, and place in the freezer. If using sticks, insert them after 30 minutes or when the mixture is firm enough for them to stand upright. Freeze until solid, 4 to 5 hours minimum.

INGREDIENTS

(Makes 6–8 three-ounce pops)

2 cups hot Vietnamese-brewed coffee or espresso

¾ cup sweetened condensed milk

TIP

A quarter teaspoonful of cream added to each pop cavity before pouring in the coffee creates a decorative swirled effect.

CHILLED CHAI

INGREDIENTS
(Makes 10–12 three-ounce pops)

2 cups cream or milk

¼ cup sugar

2 cinnamon sticks

½ teaspoon whole cloves

½ teaspoon chopped ginger

½ teaspoon whole coriander

4 green cardamom pods, crushed

½ teaspoon whole black peppercorns

5 teaspoons loose leaf black tea

2 cups water

Masala chai is served on the streets by vendors in India. Masala refers to the blend of spices, with chai meaning "tea." Masala chai became popular in India under British colonial rule: adding spices was a way to use fewer expensive tea leaves for each cup.

With the cardamom and all the spices, this pop reminds me of an Indian kulfi bar, but is much lighter and icier. Kulfi is basically Indian frozen custard: it's slightly denser than ice cream.

PREPARATION

- In a saucepan, add the milk, sugar, and spices. Slowly heat on low until it reaches a simmer. Whisk constantly for several minutes or until the sugar is completely dissolved. Remove from heat and let cool.

- In a kettle on medium-high heat, pour the water. Just before it comes to a boil, pour the water into a teapot or medium bowl over the tea leaves and let steep for five minutes.

- Pour the cooled milk mixture through a fine-mesh strainer into a medium bowl. Discard the solids. Add the spiced milk and stir thoroughly. Chill for about an hour in the refrigerator.

- Remove from refrigerator and stir in case any separation has occurred. Pour the mixture into molds, insert handles, and place in the freezer. If using sticks, insert them after 30 minutes or when the mixture is firm enough for them to stand upright. Freeze until solid, 4 to 5 hours minimum.

MOCHA

The best mochas I've ever had were down the street from my dorm during my first year of college in Berkeley. Granted, I would get them when I was procrastinating, which probably made them taste better, but they were perfect by most standards: intense, bittersweet, and rich. These pops are almost as dark and creamy.

PREPARATION

- In a saucepan on low heat, pour the milk and half-and-half. Add the cocoa, sugar, and vanilla extract and whisk to eliminate lumps and completely dissolve. Do not let the liquid boil. Once the mixture starts to steam, remove from heat. Whisk in the espresso until completely blended and chill in the refrigerator for an hour.

- Remove from the refrigerator and stir in case any separation has occurred. Pour the mixture into molds, insert handles, and place in the freezer. If using sticks, insert them after 30 minutes or when the mixture is firm enough for them to stand upright. Freeze until solid, 4 to 5 hours minimum.

INGREDIENTS
(Makes 8 three-ounce pops)

1½ cups whole milk

½ cup half-and-half

½ cup unsweetened Dutch-process cocoa powder

½ cup sugar

½ teaspoon vanilla extract

1 cup espresso coffee

POPS AROUND THE WORLD

PINEAPPLE THAI BASIL

HORCHATA

PROVENCE LAVENDER

ORANGE BLOSSOM

HALVA

LYCHEE PEACHY

ROSEMARY GRAPE

LEMON BASIL

STRAWBERRY BALSAMIC

PINEAPPLE THAI BASIL

INGREDIENTS

(Makes 8 three-ounce pops)

½ cup Thai basil leaves

1½ cups chopped fresh pineapple

½ cup sugar

¼ cup fresh-squeezed lime juice

1 cup water

Juicy pineapple combined with the clean, almost spicy taste of Thai basil is a unique tropical flavor that transports me to a hammock under a palm tree on a perfect white sand beach. You'll see what I mean when you try this. This one came about because my favorite herb farm had a surplus of Thai basil one market day—lucky me! Be sure to use Thai basil, which is available from special Asian grocers and herb vendors at farmers' markets. Regular basil won't give it that edge.

PREPARATION

- In a blender, pour all the ingredients and blend on high until the basil and pineapple are fully pulverized, with no chunks. The mixture should be a thick, pulpy juice.

- Pour the mixture into molds, insert handles, and place in the freezer. If using sticks, insert them after 30 minutes or when the mixture is firm enough for them to stand upright. Freeze until solid, 4 to 5 hours minimum.

HORCHATA

INGREDIENTS
(Makes 10–12 three-ounce pops)

4 cups almond milk

½ cup sugar

1 teaspoon cinnamon

½ teaspoon nutmeg

¼ teaspoon cloves

2 tablespoons vanilla extract

1 teaspoon almond extract

Mexico has a rich tradition of frozen pops, called paletas, *which incorporate seasonal fruit and traditional spices. These pops are an homage-with-a-twist to the paletas pushed around in little carts all over the streets of Los Angeles.* Horchata, *a creamy Mexican drink flavored with cinnamon and vanilla, isn't something you would normally find frozen on a stick, but it makes a great pop.*

PREPARATION

- In a blender, add all the ingredients and blend on high for 30 seconds until thoroughly whipped. Let the mixture rest for 15 to 20 minutes or until the top layer of froth dissolves. Pour the mixture through a fine-mesh strainer into a pitcher to remove the spice grains. Remove any remaining froth.

- Pour the mixture into molds, insert handles, and place in the freezer. If using sticks, insert them after 30 minutes or when the mixture is firm enough for them to stand upright. Freeze until solid, 4 to 5 hours minimum.

TIP
This is another great recipe to make using cinnamon sticks as handles instead of wooden sticks. It will infuse the pop with extra flavor, too.

PROVENCE LAVENDER

The scent alone makes these elegant pops aroma-therapeutic and irresistible. Sit back with one of these and let your worries melt away. They are great for baby and bridal showers with their lovely, light fragrance, and the blush color is so romantic that they are perfect for weddings, too. Or how about the perfect finale for a summer tea party?

PREPARATION

- In a small saucepan on medium heat, combine the 6 tablespoons of water and the lavender. Add 6 tablespoons sugar and stir until it is completely dissolved. Simmer for one minute, then remove from heat and let cool. Leave the lavender in the saucepan to steep and chill the mixture in the refrigerator overnight.

- Pour the chilled syrup through a fine-mesh strainer into a medium bowl and discard the lavender. In a blender, add the syrup and the remaining 6 tablespoons of sugar and 3 cups of water, and the lemon juice. Blend on high for 30 seconds.

- Pour the mixture into molds, insert handles, and place in the freezer. If using sticks, insert them after 30 minutes or when the mixture is firm enough for them to stand upright. Freeze until solid, 4 to 5 hours minimum.

INGREDIENTS
(Makes 10–12 three-ounce pops)

3 cups and 6 tablespoons water

2 tablespoons dried lavender

12 tablespoons sugar

¾ cup fresh-squeezed lemon juice

TIP
You can find dried lavender at natural food stores or other shops that sell bulk food and spices.

ORANGE BLOSSOM

Orange blossom water is used in Middle Eastern cuisine and the fragrance is delicate and alluring. It is floral, so it should be used sparingly to avoid making anything too perfumed or soapy. The water is available at specialty stores and online. This recipe is a great one to try without the sugar since it works with just the sweetness of the fruit.

PREPARATION

- In a blender, add the pineapple. Add zest and orange juice, followed by the orange blossom water and sugar. Blend on high until the pineapple is fully pureed. Let the mixture rest until any froth has dissipated, or remove the froth by spooning it off.

- Pour the mixture into molds, insert handles, and place in the freezer. If using sticks, insert them after 30 minutes or when the mixture is firm enough for them to stand upright. Freeze until solid, 4 to 5 hours minimum.

INGREDIENTS
(Makes 8–10 three-ounce pops)

2 cups chopped fresh pineapple

Zest of 1 orange

2¼ cups fresh-squeezed orange juice

1 tablespoon orange blossom water

2 tablespoons sugar

HALVA

INGREDIENTS

(Makes 8 three-ounce pops)

1 pound halva, crumbled

3 cups nonfat milk

3 tablespoons sugar

½ teaspoon sea salt

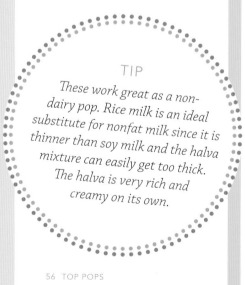

TIP

These work great as a non-dairy pop. Rice milk is an ideal substitute for nonfat milk since it is thinner than soy milk and the halva mixture can easily get too thick. The halva is very rich and creamy on its own.

Halva, meaning "sweet" in Arabic, is a candy that is served across India, Asia, the Middle East, and Eastern Europe. It has many regional variations, but I use the one that is nut butter based and common in Jewish and Eastern European cuisine. It's made from a paste of sesame or sunflower seeds and sweetened with sugar or honey, and it has a crumbly, dry texture that melts in your mouth. When an Israeli customer suggested this, I thought she was joking, but sure enough, it was a brilliant idea. These pops are nutty, creamy, and super easy to make. The hardest part is getting your hands on the halva: you can find it at Middle Eastern and Eastern European grocery shops and Jewish delis. Vanilla, chocolate, or marbled halva are all great in this recipe.

PREPARATION

• In a blender, add the halva. Add the milk, sugar, and salt and blend on high until there are no more chunks of halva and the liquid is smooth and even.

• Pour the mixture into molds, insert handles, and place in the freezer. If using sticks, insert them after 30 minutes or when the mixture is firm enough for them to stand upright. Freeze until solid, 4 to 5 hours minimum.

LYCHEE PEACHY

The flavor of the lychee is sweet, exotic, and slightly floral. Lychee lovers are devoted to their fruit and it's popular in Asia and Australia. The pairing with ripe juicy peaches gives this pop an irresistible blushing glow. Shelling the lychees is a bit of work, but it's worth it. Kids love this one, even though it's on the exotic side.

PREPARATION

- In a blender, add the lychees, peaches, sugar, and water. Blend on high until the mixture is fully pulverized, with no chunks.

- Pour the mixture into molds, insert handles, and place in the freezer. If using sticks, insert them after 30 minutes or when the mixture is firm enough for them to stand upright. Freeze until solid, 4 to 5 hours minimum.

INGREDIENTS
(Makes 10–12 three-ounce pops)

2 cups shelled, pitted, and chopped fresh lychees

1 cup chopped ripe yellow peaches

¾ cup sugar

1½ cups water

TIP

To make shelling and pitting easier, use a serrated knife to cut the lychee in half lengthwise, cutting through the skin to the pit. Pop it open and remove the skin layer. Discard the pit.

ROSEMARY GRAPE

INGREDIENTS
(Makes 10–12 three-ounce pops)

1 cup water

4 four-inch sprigs fresh rosemary

2 tablespoons sugar

4 cups Concord grape juice

These make me think of the vineyards in Chianti, where the rosemary grows like crazy. It's best to use a quality Concord grape juice to make sure these pops have the proper intensity. There's a grower at one of my local farmers' markets that bottles an excellent juice, fortunately, so I can have it all year. Save this recipe for when Concord grapes are in season and make your own grape juice for a really wonderful icy blend.

PREPARATION

- In a small saucepan on medium-low heat, add the water and rosemary. Bring to a boil and remove from heat. Add the sugar and stir until completely dissolved. Leave the rosemary in the saucepan to steep and chill the mixture overnight in the refrigerator.

- In a medium saucepan on medium-high heat, pour the grape juice and bring to a boil. Let it begin to reduce and thicken slightly by cooking for about 3 minutes. Remove from heat. Pour the rosemary syrup through a fine-mesh strainer into a medium bowl, discard the sprigs, and stir into the grape juice. Chill in the refrigerator.

- Pour the mixture into molds, insert handles, and place in the freezer. If using sticks, insert them after 30 minutes or when the mixture is firm enough for them to stand upright. Freeze until solid, 4 to 5 hours minimum.

LEMON BASIL

INGREDIENTS
(Makes 10–12 three-ounce pops)

1½ cups lemon basil leaves

1 cup lemon balm leaves

⅔ cup sugar

½ cup fresh-squeezed lemon juice

1 tablespoon lemon zest

2½ cups water

TIP
If lemon basil is hard to find, regular basil can be used. I just think the lemon basil makes them extra special, with a more complex and subtle lemon-ness. Make sure to add extra zest from one or two more lemons if you use regular basil.

This is one of my staples in the late spring and summer. Nothing beats the crispness and the clean bite of the basil flavor balanced by the lemon. These came about thanks to an herb farmer friend at one of the local markets, who insisted I take some of their lemon basil one weekend. The smell alone was enough to convince me it would make delicious pops. Although many Italians would balk at the idea of using basil for anything other than savory, this makes me think of Italy in the summer. The lemon balm also makes these calming, a great treat after dinner on a warm evening.

PREPARATION

- In a blender, add the lemon basil and lemon balm. Add the sugar, lemon juice, zest, and water. Blend for 30 seconds on medium high or until the leaves are pulverized into tiny bits.

- Slowly pour the mixture through a fine-mesh strainer into a pitcher. Depending on the size of the strainer, you might need to pour the mixture in several small batches because of the leafy pulp that will gather. Retain the pulp. Once all the liquid has been poured through the strainer, gather the pulp and press firmly through the strainer to squeeze out any remaining liquid. Let the mixture rest until any froth has dissipated, or remove the froth by spooning it off.

- Pour the mixture into molds, insert handles, and place in the freezer. If using sticks, insert them after 30 minutes or when the mixture is firm enough for them to stand upright. Freeze until solid, 4 to 5 hours minimum.

STRAWBERRY BALSAMIC

I first tried strawberries marinated in balsamic vinegar long before I moved to Italy, when a friend's mother came back from a trip with a bottle of the finest balsamic vinegar she could find in Modena, where it originated. We calculated that each drop cost about five dollars. The vinegar in this recipe, balanced by a spoonful of sugar, brings out the essence of the strawberries and gives them a robust, unique tang.

PREPARATION

• In a mixing bowl, add the strawberries and toss with the vinegar and sugar. Marinate for at least one hour at room temperature. In a blender, add the marinated strawberries, along with any liquid. Add the lemon juice and water, and blend on high for 30 seconds or until the berries are completely pulverized and the liquid is even.

• Slowly pour the mixture through a fine-mesh strainer into a pitcher. Depending on the size of the strainer, you might need to pour the mixture in several smaller batches because of the berry seeds that will gather. Discard the seeds. Let the mixture rest until any froth has dissipated, or remove the froth by spooning it off.

• Pour the mixture into molds, insert handles, and place in the freezer. If using sticks, insert them after 30 minutes or when the mixture is firm enough for them to stand upright. Freeze until solid, 4 to 5 hours minimum.

INGREDIENTS
(Makes 8–10 three-ounce pops)

1½ cups chopped strawberries

1 tablespoon balsamic vinegar

¾ cup sugar

¼ cup fresh-squeezed lemon juice

¾ cup water

KIDS' PICKS

STRAWBERRY LEMONADE

RED, WHITE, AND BLUEBERRY

CHERRY CREAM

WATERMELON LIME

BLUEBERRY LEMON

PEACHES 'N' CREAM

ROOT BEER FLOAT

MANGO LIME

STRAWBERRY LEMONADE

INGREDIENTS
(Makes 10–12 three-ounce pops)

1¾ cups chopped strawberries

½ cup fresh-squeezed lemon juice

Zest of 1 lemon

¾ cup sugar

3 cups water

TIP
Straining out all the strawberry seeds seems important to kids, who can be a bit picky.

By far, this is the most popular flavor with kids, and with adults who prefer the classics. It's just plain good. This is a tangy twist that allows the strawberries to shine through by not overpowering them with sugar, which tends to happen with many of the products on store shelves. Plus, the vibrant red color of these pops is 100 percent pure strawberry. It's hard to see why there's ever the need to add dye to strawberry pops. Let nature do the work!

PREPARATION

- In a blender, add the strawberries. Add the lemon juice and zest, and the sugar and water. Blend on high for 30 seconds or until the berries are completely pulverized and the liquid is even.

- Slowly pour the mixture through a fine-mesh strainer into a pitcher. Depending on the size of your strainer, you might need to pour the mixture in several smaller batches because of the strawberry seeds that will gather. Discard the seeds. Let the mixture rest for about half an hour until any froth has dissipated, or remove the froth by spooning it off. This froth is a tasty treat on its own!

- Pour the mixture into molds, insert handles, and place in the freezer. If using sticks, insert them after 30 minutes or when the mixture is firm enough for them to stand upright. Freeze until solid, 4 to 5 hours minimum.

RED, WHITE, AND BLUEBERRY

I was pretty obsessive about always getting a rocket pop from the ice cream truck when I was little. This pop originates from those, except you could say that this is the nonchemical version.

PREPARATION

- Red layer: In a blender, add strawberries, 1 tablespoon lemon juice, ¼ cup sugar, and ¾ cup water. Blend on high for 30 seconds or until the liquid is smooth. Slowly pour the mixture through a fine-mesh strainer into a pitcher and discard the seeds. Let the mixture rest until any froth has dissipated, or remove the froth by spooning it off. Pour the liquid into molds and place in the freezer. Insert the sticks after 15 minutes or when the pops are firm enough for them to stand upright. Freeze at least 2 hours.

- White layer: In a blender, add ½ cup lemon juice, ¼ cup sugar, and ½ cup water, and blend on high for 10 seconds or until the sugar is dissolved. Pour the mixture into molds on top of the frozen red layer. Freeze at least 2 hours.

- Blueberry layer: In a blender, add the remaining 1 tablespoon of lemon juice, the remaining ¼ cup of sugar, the remaining ¾ cup of water, and the blueberries. Blend on high for 30 seconds or until the liquid is smooth. Slowly pour the mixture through a fine-mesh strainer into a pitcher and discard the seeds. Let the mixture rest until any froth has dissipated, or remove the froth by spooning it off. Pour the mixture into molds as the final layer. Freeze at least 2 hours.

INGREDIENTS

(Makes 8 three-ounce pops)

½ cup chopped strawberries

½ cup plus 2 tablespoons fresh-squeezed lemon juice

¾ cup sugar

2 cups water

½ cup blueberries

TIP

Use wooden sticks for this pop instead of plastic handles that cover the whole base of the pop—otherwise you won't be able to pour in the second and third layers!

CHERRY CREAM

INGREDIENTS

(Makes 8 three-ounce pops)

¼ cup cherry preserves

¼ cup sugar

¼ cup pitted cherries

4 teaspoons vanilla extract

2 cups whole milk

¼ cup heavy cream

TIP

Pour a dash of the sweetened cream into the molds before adding the cherry mixture to get a bolder swirled effect.

This one's a pleaser. It has cherry going for it, which is always a popular flavor, plus the right purple-magenta color and a little creaminess. This pop is reminiscent of a Creamsicle, which is normally orange, but this similarly has a little tang and a little vanilla. I like to use sour cherries, but it's also yummy with black cherries—and really, any other kind will work just fine.

PREPARATION

- In a blender, add the preserves, ¼ cup of the sugar, cherries, vanilla extract, and milk. Blend on high until the cherries are fully pulverized, about 30 seconds. Let stand.

- In a saucepan on low heat, add the remaining ¼ cup of sugar and the cream, and stir until the sugar has completely dissolved. Do not allow it to boil. Let cool to room temperature, about 30 minutes. Add the cream to the blender and blend on low until the two mixtures are swirled together but not completely blended.

- Pour the mixture into molds, insert handles, and place in the freezer. If using sticks, insert them after 30 minutes or when the mixture is firm enough for them to stand upright. Freeze until solid, 4 to 5 hours minimum.

WATERMELON LIME

This is the most refreshing, light, low-sugar summer classic. There is no mistaking fresh watermelon for the artificial candy flavor so many people associate with any kind of watermelon treat. Real watermelon is subtle, delicate, and flawlessly sweet. Show your kids that the real deal is so much better. A dash of sugar brings out the flavor of the fruit in this case, but it is by no means necessary if you prefer to play this one on a healthier note.

PREPARATION

- In a blender, add the watermelon, the lime juice and zest, then the agave or sugar, and finally a dash of salt. Blend on high until the watermelon is completely liquefied.

- Pour the mixture into molds, insert handles, and place in the freezer. If using sticks, insert them after 30 minutes or when the mixture is firm enough for them to stand upright. Freeze until solid, 4 to 5 hours minimum.

INGREDIENTS
(Makes 10–12 three-ounce pops)

6 cups cubed seedless watermelon (about 1 four-pound watermelon)

2 tablespoons fresh-squeezed lime juice

Zest of 2 limes

¼ cup agave nectar or sugar

Dash of sea salt

TIP
Depending on your blender, you might want to mash up the watermelon with a spoon before you put it in the blender to get it to start blending more easily.

BLUEBERRY LEMON

INGREDIENTS
(Makes 12–14 three-ounce pops)

1½ cups blueberries

⅓ cup fresh-squeezed lemon juice

Zest of 1 lemon

⅔ cup sugar

3½ cups water

Sadly, despite numerous requests from enthusiastic kids, blue isn't a color that exists in nature, and that's the only kind of dye I generally use in my pops. However, most kids seem to think the dark purple color of these pops is a pretty nice compromise. Color aside, the antioxidants from the blueberries can't be beat, and the flavor is just perfect when you get ripe berries at the height of the season.

PREPARATION

- In a blender, add all the ingredients and blend on high until the blueberries are fully pulverized. Let the mixture rest until any froth has dissipated, or remove the froth by spooning it off.

- Pour the mixture into molds, insert handles, and place in the freezer. If using sticks, insert them after 30 minutes or when the mixture is firm enough for them to stand upright. Freeze until solid, 4 to 5 hours minimum.

INGREDIENTS

(Makes 8 three-ounce pops)

4 ripe yellow peaches

3 tablespoons vanilla extract

5 tablespoons sugar

1 teaspoon fresh-squeezed lemon juice

1 cup water

2 cups half-and-half

TIP

You can also use nectarines for this recipe. Their high acid content may give them a stronger flavor than the peaches that might be available.

PEACHES 'N' CREAM

It's often hard to find supermarket peaches that are remotely ripe and ready to eat. Getting them at a farmers' market is really worth it: the grower has ripened them and handled them properly.

The tangier the peach, the more intense the pop. Also, leaving the skins on the peaches gives them some added color, but you can remove the skins if you prefer.

PREPARATION

- Slice the peaches in half and remove the pits. In a medium saucepan on medium low heat, add the peaches, 2 tablespoons of the vanilla extract, and 3 tablespoons of the sugar, along with the lemon juice and water. Stir frequently and cook until the peaches are completely soft and a thick syrup has formed. Remove from heat and let cool.

- In a small saucepan on low heat, add the remaining vanilla extract and sugar, and the half-and-half, and stir until the sugar has completely dissolved. Cool in the refrigerator for 30 minutes.

- In a blender, add the cream mixture and the cooked peaches and blend on low until the two mixtures are swirled together but not completely blended.

- Pour the mixture into molds, insert handles, and place in the freezer. If using sticks, insert them after 20 minutes or when the mixture is firm enough for them to stand upright. Freeze until solid, 4 to 5 hours minimum.

ROOT BEER FLOAT

You can make these pops in a jiffy as a sweet treat before a playdate or summer picnic. The hardest part is waiting for the root beer to get flat because the foam it creates with the ice cream doesn't freeze well. Use a good specialty cane-sugar-sweetened root beer for the best results. Some of the more generic brands are little flavorless. I have a friend who is working on a home-brewed version that will put these over the top.

PREPARATION

- In a pitcher, pour the root beer and refrigerate for an hour to let it get flat and cold.

- In the bottom of each mold, pour 1 teaspoon of the root beer. Slowly smear 1 teaspoon of the ice cream on top. Make sure the ice cream is frozen very hard so that it does not immediately melt into the root beer. Pour the remaining root beer into a bowl and slowly add the remaining ice cream. Stir gently until mixed and spoon off any foam that forms.

- Pour the mixture into molds, insert handles, and place in the freezer. If using sticks, insert them after 10 minutes or when the mixture is firm enough for them to stand upright. The ice cream will help them to stand up quickly. Freeze until solid, 4 to 5 hours minimum.

INGREDIENTS
(Makes 6 three-ounce pops)

1½ cups root beer

¾ cup vanilla ice cream

TIP
You can substitute other sodas here, such as cherry Coke or orange soda.

MANGO LIME

These pops are best with super-ripe mangos. You can get away with not adding sugar if the mangos are sweet enough. This is a classic paleta flavor, and the balance of sweet and sour gets it just right. The sunny orange color with specks of lime zest makes these one of the prettier pops.

PREPARATION

- In a blender, add all the ingredients and blend to a smooth, thick consistency. Flecks of lime zest will still be visible in the mixture.

- Pour the mixture into molds, insert handles, and place in the freezer. If using sticks, insert them after 15 minutes or when the mixture is firm enough for them to stand upright. Freeze until solid, 4 to 5 hours minimum.

INGREDIENTS

(Makes 8–10 three-ounce pops)

2 cups peeled, pitted, and sliced mango (about two mangos)

3 tablespoons fresh-squeezed lime juice

1 teaspoon lime zest

1½ cups water

½ cup sugar

HOLIDAYS ON ICE

CRANBERRY CLOVE

PUMPKIN PIE

PERSIMMON SPICE PUDDING POP

CHOCOLATE PEPPERMINT

NEW YEAR'S EVE RASPBERRY BUBBLY (WITH PROSECCO)

CRANBERRY CLOVE

INGREDIENTS

(Makes 10–12 three-ounce pops)

4 cups unsweetened 100 percent cranberry juice

1⅔ cups sugar

2 cups water

2 heaping teaspoons whole cloves

My uncle's cranberry sauce is one of my favorite parts of Thanksgiving—it's too good to eat just one night of the year. This captures the essence in frozen form. As a pop, the combination of tart cranberries and spicy clove is a fantastic palate cleanser after a heavy holiday meal.

PREPARATION

* In a medium saucepan on low heat, add all the ingredients and stir until the sugar is completely dissolved. Simmer for 10 minutes. Remove from heat and let stand for one hour. Pour the mixture through a fine-mesh strainer into a pitcher to remove the cloves.

* Pour the mixture into molds, insert handles, and place in the freezer. If using sticks, insert them after 20 minutes or when the mixture is firm enough for them to stand upright. Freeze until solid, 4 to 5 hours minimum.

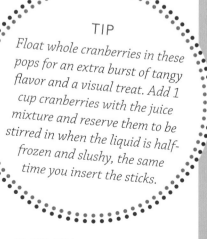

TIP
Float whole cranberries in these pops for an extra burst of tangy flavor and a visual treat. Add 1 cup cranberries with the juice mixture and reserve them to be stirred in when the liquid is half-frozen and slushy, the same time you insert the sticks.

INGREDIENTS

(Makes 10–12 three-ounce pops)

3 cups whole milk

½ cup brown sugar

1 teaspoon vanilla extract

½ teaspoon cinnamon

½ teaspoon ginger

½ teaspoon cloves

½ teaspoon nutmeg

Pinch of sea salt

1½ cups pumpkin puree, homemade or canned

TIP

For a fun touch, freeze a layer of lightly whipped whipping cream in the bottom of each mold. Freeze for 2 hours or until solid, and pour the pumpkin mixture on top.

PUMPKIN PIE

I was supposed to make pie for Thanksgiving a couple of years ago, but it was crazy hot in Los Angeles so I dreaded turning on the oven. I made the filling, and thought I'd give it a shot and try freezing it into pops instead because the consistency is like the other creamy pudding pops. What a cool (no pun intended) way to enjoy this fall tradition.

PREPARATION

- In a medium saucepan on medium heat, add the milk, brown sugar, vanilla extract, ginger, cloves, nutmeg, and salt. Whisk vigorously to eliminate lumps and completely dissolve the sugar. Bring the mixture to a boil and reduce to low heat. Let cool for 30 minutes.

- In a blender, add the pumpkin puree and pour the cooled milk mixture over it. Blend for 30 seconds or until thoroughly blended and perfectly smooth in consistency.

- Pour the mixture into molds, insert handles, and place in the freezer. If using sticks, insert them after 20 minutes or when the mixture is firm enough for them to stand upright. Freeze until solid, 4 to 5 hours minimum.

PERSIMMON SPICE PUDDING POP

Persimmons are a winter fruit that is under-used by most Americans. I learned to love them in Italy, where they serve ripe persimmons with nothing but a spoon for dessert. When ripe, the pulp is basically gelatinous custard that you can scoop out of the skin—Hachiya persimmons are especially soft. Adding the spices makes for a zesty treat.

PREPARATION

- In a medium saucepan on medium heat, add the milk, brown sugar, vanilla extract, cinnamon stick, cloves, allspice, ginger, and salt. Whisk vigorously to eliminate lumps and completely dissolve the sugar. Reduce the heat to low when the mixture starts to boil. Let cool for 30 minutes. Pour the mixture through a fine-mesh strainer into a medium bowl to remove the spice grains and cinnamon stick.

- Peel and remove the pulp from the persimmons. In a blender, add the persimmon pulp and the cooled milk mixture. Puree for 30 seconds or until thoroughly blended and perfectly smooth in consistency.

- Pour the mixture into molds, insert handles, and place in the freezer. If using sticks, insert them after 30 minutes or when the mixture is firm enough for them to stand upright. Freeze until solid, 4 to 5 hours minimum.

INGREDIENTS
(Makes 10–12 three-ounce pops)

1½ cups whole milk

½ cup brown sugar

½ teaspoon vanilla extract

1 cinnamon stick

½ teaspoon whole cloves

½ teaspoon whole allspice

¼ teaspoon ground ginger

Dash of sea salt

3 cups fresh, very ripe Hachiya persimmon pulp (about 1½ persimmons)

CHOCOLATE PEPPERMINT

These started out as a winter pop: I used candy canes instead of wooden sticks to make them more special for parties. But they became so popular that I now make them year-round. The peppermint makes them extra cooling and ideal for beating the summer heat.

PREPARATION

* In a large saucepan on low heat, add all the ingredients. Whisk frequently and vigorously to remove any lumps. Do not allow the mixture to boil and begin to reduce. Once the sugar has completely dissolved and the liquid is well blended, remove from heat. Chill in refrigerator for at least 30 minutes.

* Pour the mixture into molds, insert handles, and place in the freezer. If using sticks, insert them after 30 minutes or when the mixture is firm enough for them to stand upright. Freeze until solid, 4 to 5 hours minimum.

INGREDIENTS

(Makes 10–12 three-ounce pops)

4 cups milk

1 cup unsweetened Dutch-process cocoa powder

½ cup sugar

1 teaspoon peppermint oil

INGREDIENTS

(Makes 10 three-ounce pops)

⅔ cup fresh raspberries

½ cup sugar

⅓ cup fresh-squeezed lemon juice

2½ cup water

½ cup Prosecco

NEW YEAR'S EVE RASPBERRY BUBBLY (WITH PROSECCO)

These are the ultimate festive and romantic treats. They're perfect for ringing in the New Year, and I've also done them for Valentine's Day dinners. Nothing says romance like luscious berries and a little bit of bubbly. The intense rose color of these alone might make you swoon. If you prefer, you can substitute champagne or any other sparkling white wine for the Prosecco. I like the fruitiness of Prosecco, plus, I'm an Italophile.

PREPARATION

- In a blender, add the raspberries, sugar, lemon juice, and water. Blend on high for 20 seconds. Add the Prosecco and let the fizz settle for a moment. Blend on low for just a few seconds. Let the mixture rest until any froth has dissipated, or remove the froth by spooning it off. Pour the mixture through a fine-mesh strainer into a pitcher and discard the berry seeds.

- Pour the mixture into molds, insert handles, and place in the freezer. If using sticks, insert them after one hour or when the mixture is firm enough for them to stand upright. Freeze until solid, at least 5 hours. Due to the alcohol content, these pops take longer to freeze.

TIPSY POPS

PIÑA COLADA

SPIKED APPLE CIDER

MOJITO

LIMONCELLO

WHITE PEACH AMARETTO

CHOCOLATE GRAND MARNIER

WATERMELON MINT JULEP

MANGO CHILI MARGARITA

PIÑA COLADA

I had my first virgin piña colada on a family vacation to Mexico when I was about eight, and I've been hooked ever since. These are perfectly rich, thanks to the coconut milk. Serve them by the pool or at any warm-weather fiesta and your guests will be ready to party.

INGREDIENTS
(Makes 8-10 three-ounce pops)

2 cups chopped fresh pineapple

2 cups coconut milk

3 tablespoons vanilla extract

⅔ cup sugar

½ cup light or white rum

¼ cup shredded unsweetened coconut

PREPARATION

- In a blender, add the pineapple, coconut milk, vanilla extract, sugar, and rum. Blend on high for 30 seconds or until the pineapple is fully blended and no longer chunky. Stir in the shredded coconut and pulse to mix thoroughly.

- Pour the mixture into molds, insert handles, and place in the freezer. If using sticks, insert them after 30 minutes or when the mixture is firm enough for them to stand upright. Freeze until solid, at least 5 hours. Due to the alcohol content, these pops take longer to freeze.

SPIKED APPLE CIDER

INGREDIENTS

(Makes 10–12 three-ounce pops)

4 cups fresh, cold-pressed apple juice

½ cup brown sugar

1 tablespoon cinnamon

½ teaspoon whole cloves

½ teaspoon ground ginger

½ cup brandy

These pops can be made with a number of kinds of liquor. Rum and brandy both complement the apple sweetness quite well. Using fresh apple juice gives these much more flavor than the standard juice that comes from concentrate. This is a fun way for those of us in temperate Los Angeles to feel like it's fall, even when it's 80 degrees in November!

PREPARATION

- In a saucepan on medium-low heat, add the apple juice, sugar, cinnamon, cloves, and ginger. Heat until the mixture starts steaming. Turn down to low just before the mixture comes to a boil. Let the mixture cool to room temperature for 30 minutes. Stir in the brandy and pour through a fine-mesh strainer into a pitcher to remove the spice grains.

- Pour the mixture into molds, insert handles, and place in the freezer. If using sticks, insert them after one hour or when the mixture is firm enough for them to stand upright. Freeze until solid, at least 5 hours. Due to the alcohol content, these pops take longer to freeze.

MOJITO

The mojito originated in Cuba and consists of macerated limes and mint with sugar cane, set off with a splash of soda and, of course, a generous hit of rum. Nowadays, mojitos are almost as common in bars and restaurants as Bud Light. They hit the scene in the late 1990s and quickly became the "it" drink, with endless variations on the ingredients. This pop is more of a purist's take. It's great with or without the rum. The splashy green color is fun at parties, and the combination of lime and mint is the ultimate cooldown in the heat.

PREPARATION

- In a blender, add the mint and then the lime juice, sugar, rum, and water. Blend for 30 seconds on medium high until the mint is pulverized into tiny bits.

- Slowly pour the mixture through a fine-mesh strainer into a pitcher. Depending on the size of the strainer, you might need to pour the liquid in several smaller batches because of the mint pulp that will gather. Retain the pulp. Once all the liquid has been poured through the strainer, firmly press the mint pulp to squeeze out any remaining juices. Let the mixture rest until any froth has dissipated, or remove the froth by spooning it off.

- Pour the mixture into molds, insert handles, and place in the freezer. If using sticks, insert them after one hour or when the mixture is firm enough for them to stand upright. Freeze until solid, at least 5 hours. Due to the alcohol content, these pops take longer to freeze.

INGREDIENTS
(Makes 10–12 three-ounce pops)

2 cups fresh mint leaves

½ cup fresh-squeezed lime juice

⅔ cup sugar

½ cup light or white rum

2½ cups water

LIMONCELLO

Italy's Amalfi Coast is every bit as picturesque as people say. Plus, they make the finest Limoncello in those towns, so it wins for that alone. Limoncello is served chilled, but these pops take that up a notch, and it works very well. These are a stylish way to top off a garden dinner party.

PREPARATION

- In a blender, add all the ingredients and blend on high for 30 seconds or until the sugar is completely dissolved. Chill for about 30 minutes, allowing any froth to dissipate, or remove the froth by spooning it off.

- Pour the mixture into molds, insert handles, and place in the freezer. If using sticks, insert them after 45 minutes or when the mixture is firm enough for them to stand upright. Freeze until solid, at least 5 hours. Due to the alcohol content, these pops take longer to freeze.

INGREDIENTS
(Makes 6–8 three-ounce pops)

1 cup fresh-squeezed lemon juice

1 cup water

½ cup sugar

Zest of two lemons

⅓ cup Limoncello

TIP
You can blend in fresh thyme, mint, verbena, or other light herbs to give this pop a special twist.

WHITE PEACH AMARETTO

INGREDIENTS
(Makes 10–12 three-ounce pops)

4 ripe white peaches

2 cups water

1 cup sugar

¼ cup fresh-squeezed lemon juice

½ cup amaretto

2 teaspoons almond extract

This versatile recipe can use any variety of peaches or nectarines, or a combo of both. Use whatever varietals are at the peak of their season for the juiciest and most flavorful results. In the last few years, the intensity of American white peaches has gotten much stronger, but still, the tastiest white peaches I've ever eaten were in Italy. The bitter almond is such an Italian flavoring that it works perfectly alongside the peach. The color of these pops is light and lovely.

PREPARATION

- Cut the peaches in half and remove the pits. Partially remove the peels, leaving about half for color. In a medium saucepan on medium-low heat, add the peaches, water, sugar, and lemon juice. Cook on low and stir frequently until the liquid becomes syrupy and the peaches are soft and mushy. Remove from heat and let cool.

- In a blender, add the peach mixture, amaretto, and almond extract and blend on high for 30 seconds, or until the mixture is completely smooth.

- Pour the mixture into molds, insert handles, and place in the freezer. If using sticks, insert them after 30 minutes or when the mixture is firm enough for them to stand upright. Freeze until solid, at least 5 hours. Due to the alcohol content, these pops take longer to freeze.

CHOCOLATE GRAND MARNIER

Could it get any more decadent than this? My French neighbor at the farmers' market, who makes the most incredible chocolate croissants I've ever had (including the ones in Paris that I thought were the best for many years), told me to try this combo in his very French way. He was right, of course. He knows his chocolate. I love seeing this guy reluctantly savor his pops on Sunday morning. He was skeptically French about them at first, but he's now a convert.

PREPARATION

- In a medium saucepan on low heat, add the milk, cocoa, orange zest, and sugar. Whisk vigorously to eliminate any lumps and completely dissolve the sugar. Do not let the mixture boil and begin to reduce. Once all the ingredients are incorporated, remove from heat. Chill in the refrigerator for an hour.

- Whisk in the Grand Marnier and pour the mixture into molds. Insert handles and place in the freezer. If using sticks, insert them after 30 minutes or when the mixture is firm enough for them to stand upright. Freeze until solid, at least 5 hours. Due to the alcohol content, these pops take longer to freeze.

INGREDIENTS
(Makes 10–12 three-ounce pops)

3 cups whole milk

½ cup unsweetened Dutch-process cocoa powder

Zest of two oranges

½ cup sugar

⅔ cup Grand Marnier

WATERMELON MINT JULEP

INGREDIENTS
(Makes 10–12 three-ounce pops)

6 cups cubed, seedless watermelon (about 1 four-pound watermelon)

¼ cup sugar

2 tablespoons fresh-squeezed lime juice

½ cup bourbon

Pinch of sea salt

2 tablespoons chopped fresh mint

It's difficult to get the right balance between the watermelon, which actually has a pretty subtle flavor, and the mint, which can easily overpower it. The sea salt helps bring out the flavor of the watermelon in this recipe. Also, I learned the hard way that green and red-pink make brown when I over-blended this for a private order. Using the mint as flecks will give just the right essence, and it's much more attractive.

PREPARATION

- In a blender, add the watermelon, sugar, lime juice, bourbon, and salt. Blend on high until the mixture has an even liquid consistency.

- Pour the liquid into molds, insert handles, and place in the freezer. After 30 minutes, or when the pops are half-frozen and slushy, stir a pinch of the mint into each mold to suspend it evenly throughout each pop. Replace the handles, or, if using wooden sticks, insert them now, when the mixture is firm enough for them to stand upright. Freeze until solid, 5 hours minimum. Due to the alcohol content, these pops take longer to freeze.

MANGO CHILI MARGARITA

This pop is not exactly a margarita, but it's close. That kick of chili heat is lots of fun and a nod to the Mexican tradition. If you can get Ataulfo or Manila mangos, go for it: they have fantastic flavor and the flesh is buttery, rather than stringy like other varietals.

PREPARATION

- In a blender, add all the ingredients and blend on high for 30 seconds or until the mixture is completely smooth, with no remaining chunks of mango.

- Pour the mixture into molds, insert handles, and place in the freezer. If using sticks, insert them after 30 minutes or when the mixture is firm enough for them to stand upright. Freeze until solid, at least 5 hours. Due to the alcohol content, these pops take longer to freeze.

INGREDIENTS

(Makes 8–10 three-ounce pops)

2 cups peeled, pitted, and sliced mango (about 2 mangos)

3 tablespoons fresh-squeezed lime juice

1 teaspoon lime zest

1½ cups water

½ cup sugar

½ cup silver or blanco tequila

Dash of chili powder

POP THERAPY

CUCUMBER LIME

MEYER LEMON GINGER

APPLE FENUGREEK

WHEATGRASS CITRUS

LEMON MINT

CUCUMBER LIME

INGREDIENTS

(Makes 8–10 three-ounce pops)

2 peeled cucumbers

⅓ cup fresh-squeezed lime juice

½ teaspoon lime zest

¾ cup sugar

1 cup water

Chilled cucumber water is always a fun part of going to my favorite spa. It's so simple, but it makes sipping water much more special. I hope these pops will give the illusion of transporting you to a relaxing retreat. Cucumbers are hydrating and they're an anti-inflammatory, but resist the temptation to put the pops on your eyes—the lime won't feel too good.

These are a chic choice for bridal and baby showers. Plus, they're thirst quenching, so they're great for sporting events like tennis and softball games.

PREPARATION

* Cut the cucumbers in half lengthwise and remove most of the seeds. Cut them lengthwise again into quarter spears. In a blender, add the cucumbers, lime juice, lime zest, sugar, and water. Blend on high until evenly blended to a very fine pulp.

* Pour the mixture into molds, insert handles, and place in the freezer. If using sticks, insert them after 30 minutes or when the mixture is firm enough for them to stand upright. Freeze until solid, 4 to 5 hours minimum.

MEYER LEMON GINGER

INGREDIENTS

(Makes 12–14 three-ounce pops)

¾ cup fresh-squeezed
Meyer lemon juice

Zest of 1 Meyer lemon

¾ cup sugar

3½ cups water

2 tablespoons peeled and
chopped fresh ginger

Lemon ginger pops are the perfect palate cleanser, which was how this recipe came to be. As it turns out, this flavor combo is also great for treating everything from sore throats to tummy aches and nausea. I was touched when a customer ordered them for a friend who was going through chemotherapy. Pregnant women have been known to get addicted to these—one woman even ordered them to bring to the hospital during her delivery! I started calling them "pregnancy pops" after I survived my first trimester on them.

Meyer lemons make these pops tangy but less tart than standard lemons. The zest from Meyer lemon skins also adds a delicate, sophisticated fragrance and a yellow spark of color that's sure to please.

PREPARATION

- In a blender, add all the ingredients and puree for 30 seconds. Pour the mixture through a fine-mesh strainer into a pitcher, pressing hard on the solids to squeeze out as much liquid as possible. Let the mixture rest until any froth has dissipated, or remove the froth by spooning it off. Chill in the refrigerator for 10 minutes.

- Pour the mixture into molds, insert handles, and place in the freezer. If using sticks, insert them after 45 minutes or when the mixture is firm enough for them to stand upright. Freeze until solid, 4 to 5 hours minimum.

APPLE FENUGREEK

When my daughter was born, I got addicted to the "Mother's Milk" brand of lactation-promoting teas with fenugreek, mainly because I liked the taste. As it got warm, drinking hot tea became less and less appealing, so I created my own chilly interpretation of the flavors in those teas. My first attempt at this recipe was actually more of a savory soup, because I was shocked to learn that they need just a little bit of fenugreek in comparison to the other spices.

PREPARATION

- In a medium saucepan on medium-low heat, add all the ingredients and simmer for 10 minutes, stirring occasionally. Remove from heat and chill in the refrigerator for 15 minutes. Pour the mixture through a fine-mesh strainer into a pitcher to remove the spice grains and lemongrass stalks.

- Pour the mixture into molds, insert handles, and place in the freezer. If using sticks, insert them after 30 minutes or when the mixture is firm enough for them to stand upright. Freeze until solid, 4 to 5 hours minimum.

INGREDIENTS

(Makes 8–10 three-ounce pops)

4 cups fresh cold-pressed apple juice

6 tablespoons whole fennel seed

¼ cup whole anise seed

1 teaspoon whole fenugreek

2 teaspoons whole coriander

2 six-inch lemongrass stalks

Pinch of whole allspice

4 teaspoons sugar

WHEATGRASS CITRUS

Even if you're not a big wheatgrass fan, you'll like this pop. It will energize you in no time. Providing chlorophyll, amino acids, and vitamins, wheatgrass is a true super food. You can usually find it at health food stores either in grass form, as a fresh juice, or as frozen juice tablets.

PREPARATION

- In a blender, add all the ingredients and blend on high for 15 seconds or until the juices are thoroughly mixed. Let the mixture rest until any froth has dissipated, or remove the froth by spooning it off.

- Pour the mixture into molds, insert handles, and place in the freezer. If using sticks, insert them after 30 minutes or when the mixture is firm enough for them to stand upright. Freeze until solid, 4 to 5 hours minimum.

INGREDIENTS

(Makes 8 three-ounce pops)

¼ cup wheatgrass juice

1½ cups fresh-squeezed orange juice

¼ cup agave nectar

3 teaspoons fresh-squeezed lime juice

3 teaspoons fresh-squeezed lemon juice

Zest of two lemons

LEMON MINT

INGREDIENTS

(Makes 10–12 three-ounce pops)

2 cups fresh mint leaves

½ cup fresh-squeezed lemon juice

2½ cups water

⅔ cup sugar

Zest of 2 lemons

Lemon and mint are such a refreshing duo. The mint is cooling and soothing, making these a great alternative digestif on a hot summer night. This simple pairing also works great if your tummy isn't feeling so good.

PREPARATION

- In a blender, add all the ingredients and blend for 30 seconds on medium high until the mint is pulverized into tiny bits.

- Pour the mixture through a fine-mesh strainer into a pitcher. Depending on the size of the strainer, you might need to pour the mixture in several smaller batches because of the mint pulp that will gather. Retain this pulp. Once all the liquid has been poured through the strainer, firmly press the mint pulp to squeeze out any remaining liquid. Let the mixture rest until any froth has dissipated, or remove the froth by spooning it off.

- Pour the mixture into molds, insert handles, and place in the freezer. If using sticks, insert them after 30 minutes or when the mixture is firm enough for them to stand upright. Freeze until solid, 4 to 5 hours minimum.

TIP
For added visual appeal, chop extra mint leaves and stir a pinch into each pop mold after 30 minutes, or when the pops are slushy, to suspend the leaves throughout.

INDEX

FOR LILA

TOP POPS. Copyright © 2012 by becker&mayer! LLC. Text © 2012 by Emily Zaiden. All rights reserved. Printed in China. For information, address St. Martin's Press, 175 Fifth Avenue, New York, NY 10010.

www.stmartins.com

Photographs copyright © 2012 by Lara Ferroni

Book design: Rosebud Eustace
Editorial: Kjersti Egerdahl and Dana Youlin
Photo shoot production: Shayna Ian

Library of Congress Cataloging-in-Publication Data Available Upon Request.

ISBN 978-1-250-00426-0

First Edition: May 2012

10 9 8 7 6 5 4 3 2 1

Top Pops is produced by becker&mayer!, Bellevue, Washington
www.beckermayer.com